New York Times Bestselling Author
RANDY GAGE

The ABCs of MLM

Copyright © 2024, Prosperity Factory, Inc.

All rights reserved. No part of this book can be reproduced or transmitted in any form or by any means, electronic or mechanical, including photocopying, recording, or by any information storage and retrieval system, without permission from the publisher. This book is also available in volume discounts.

Published by Prosperity Factory, Inc.
PO Box 693008
Miami, FL 33269-3008
https://randygage.com/

First Edition. Printed in the United States of America

Library of Congress Catalog-in-Publication Date March 5, 2024
Gage, Randy
The ABCs of MLM
Library of Congress Control Number: 2024901888
ISBN: 978-0-9979482-3-3

BUSINESS & ECONOMICS/ Marketing/Direct

Here's what top leaders and founders in the profession say about *The ABCs of MLM*:

"If you want to fast-track launching your business, this is the book for you. Short. Easy. Filled with humorous examples and packed with life-changing business principles. Love it. A masterpiece!"
— **Hilde & Ørjan Saele**

"This is a real life 'how to' book that all new and seasoned distributors and consultants need to read and apply. Randy delivers the field guide for creating the life of your dreams. You'll want each member of your team to have a copy!"
— **Jordan Adler**

"An indispensable guide for anyone venturing into the world of network marketing. With insightful wisdom and actionable strategies, it is practical and empowering, but a fun read, too, which makes it easy to absorb, even for those who don't like reading!"
— **Wes Linden**

"Network marketing is a unique business model and few people who start in the profession really understand it. Randy's track record of extraordinary success and his ability to communicate make this the perfect tool for breaking down the principles that build and drive success."
— **Dana Collins**

"Sometimes you're going to struggle, get down, or face challenges. When you do, this book will get you back in the game!"
— **Erick Gamio**

"Something that I can give every new builder on my team so that they can have a blueprint of how the business works."
— **Eugene Hong**

"Randy has created a practical manual that presents what we need to know and, above all, what we must do to propel our business towards success."
— **Juan Carlos Barrios**

"If every new distributor read, understood, and implemented this advice… We would soon need another planet to recruit from!"
— **Peter Andreas Sørensen**

"Randy has been a thought leader for more than four decades and has created a timely and much-needed guide on how to succeed in MLM now and beyond. Read and grow *your* business."
— **John Solleder**

"A brilliant resource to help your team move from hope to belief!"
— **Ann Feinstein**

"Randy did an excellent job creating a book for those beginning their network marketing entrepreneurship. I appreciate how he sets the expectations up front so that readers know exactly what it takes to succeed in the profession."
— **JJ Birden**

"What I love most about this book is that you get amazing, straight-to-the-point advice on what is working right now."
— **Jeremiah Bradley**

"An incredible book that should be read by all team members in the industry!"
— **Dan Higginson**

"If I had the information in this book in my first year, I would not have lost six years in my direct sales journey."
— **Nahsan Simsek**

"Great leaders have a superpower: the ability to transmit a compelling vision to your team. This book helps you do that!"
— **Raul Tufik**

"Every person should read this book immediately after signing up, and every leader should reread it always to remember what it takes to get their new people launched."
— **Michael Smith**

"If you have a dream, this book will help you build the faith you need to achieve your dream. And never give up until you do. Thank you, Randy!"
— **Stoil Palhutev**

"Are you looking for a training tool to build a big direct-selling organization? This book is what you are looking for! Not only read it: live it and promote it. AMAZING!"
— **Payam Moghim Eslam**

"A provocative book that will challenge you to rethink some of your core assumptions about what it takes to align people for real success"
— **Jeff Higginson**

"The question 'What should be the first book I give my new distributor?' is settled. This is it! The definite guide to the crucial first steps in the business and it should be in the starter kit of every single company in the world. This book will save millions of dreams of being lost!"
— **Jose Lopez**

"He's done it again! In this book Randy leads the reader from concept to implementation in an intuitive manner that Apple thought only they held the keys to."
— **Travis Parry**

"This is the best book. It contains Randy's wise guidance and is needed so much! I will recommend to everyone on my team"
— **Lily Rosales**

"Randy Gage is our greatest guide. This book is the best foundation for those who want to start big and with a clear vision"
— **Luca Melloni**

Dedication

To the dreamers crazy enough to believe that they have the power to alter the trajectory of the universe, even if it's only by a millimeter.

Introduction: The Mystery Explained

Frequently I get asked for the secret of success in our business: how to unravel the mystery of building a massive team with huge volume that creates a legacy income. The so-called mystery is simply a case of the successful people refusing to run away and quit when faced with the same challenges that scare away the non-successful. If we insist on trying to quantify some secret about the process, allow me to distill it down to one fundamental truth…

You got into this crazy profession because of *hope*. Whether you stay in and become successful will come down to *belief*.

People join our biz because they *hope* they will qualify for that free bonus car, win the luxury trips, find a rewarding new career, and have those meaty commission checks deposited into their account every week. They hope the business will work. And as long as that hope stays alive, they stay active. If that hope dies, they drop out. This means that every new distributor in your team is a flight risk to quit.

Until one specific dynamic happens…

Their hope is transformed into *belief*. We call this process "getting someone over the line." Because once they cross that line from hope to belief, there's a disproportionate chance that they will never quit. Which leads us to this book, why I wrote it, and what it can mean for you. The most important objective is to get *you* over the line. To share with you the simple but vital actions to take at the beginning of your career to get you into the belief column as quickly as possible.

There are not many people on Earth who have been able to create the magnitude of success I've produced in leveraged sales/network marketing. Over the course of my career as a distributor, coach, company executive, and consultant (but principally as a distributor), I've

THE ABCS OF MLMS

seen the business from every perspective and been part of teams that have produced literally tens of billions of dollars in revenue. Those results transformed my life, taking me from a high school dropout to wealth and prosperity. Ironically, I struggled for the first five years of my career, buying products and tools, attending event after event, losing money every month. Even after I had become a bit profitable, it was still a couple years more before I went from hope to belief.

Looking back, I have no idea how I held onto hope for that long. Probably because I was too ignorant to know any better, or maybe because the alternative of giving up on my dream was too depressing to even consider. One thing I do know for sure…

People in today's culture will never hang around as long as I did. You probably won't and most of your team won't as well. Which is exactly where this book comes in. By now you already know that it costs a tenth the price of other books on network marketing.

Why?

Because I'm not writing this to make money but offer you the most powerful tool available to get both you and your team over the line in weeks instead of years. We've priced the book so you can buy them by the dozen, leaders can buy them by the hundreds, and companies can buy them by the tens of thousands. My hope is that companies will include them in their distributor kits, or leaders will buy them in enough bulk so that every person who joins the team will read this book as part of their new distributor orientation process. I hope you'll read Book One before you contact your first candidate, so your belief in what you have to offer is rock solid.

Note: However, if you tell your sponsor you're waiting to contact people until after you've finished reading that section, you've defeated the entire purpose of the book and you're practicing self-sabotage. You can scarf down the Scooby snacks of Book One in fifteen minutes or less. Use it for a catalyst, not an excuse.

This simple little book will teach you the foundation for growing a successful team: the mindset required and the fundamental actions that set the DNA of your organization in your first few weeks so you'll have the proper foundation to create the team and business of your dreams.

Interesting side note: Many have asked why I titled the book using the term MLM, which I abandoned many years ago—preferring terms such as direct selling, network marketing, or leveraged sales which have less emotional baggage. Here's why…

Decades ago, my friend Mark Yarnell created a cassette tape (Google it) to educate new distributors what to expect when they first joined the business. The cassette prepared them for things like dropouts, rejection, and no-shows—but more importantly—explained why the result was worth the challenges you face along the way. The tape was titled *The ABCs of MLM*, and since this book has a similar goal, I've resurrected the title to pay homage to Mark, one of the true OGs of our profession.

This book can have a profound impact on your business, creating a yet bigger impact in your life. Really. Please make the most of it!

Randy Gage
Miami Beach, Florida
January 2024

Book One

The Red Pill or the Blue Pill?

Do You Have Any Idea What You Just Did?

Do you realize what just happened? You innocently whipped out your credit card, placed an activation order, and now you've started a chain reaction of tiny ripple effects that could culminate in a reality-altering outcome. You have officially joined the society of crazy people who believe dreams are worth chasing.

What's next?

Probably the most exciting thrill ride of your career. Really. Because you've made a fantastic choice. You've chosen what is arguably the premier option of becoming a social entrepreneur. Social entrepreneurs are dedicated to building business in a way that empowers themselves and others, serving the greater good.

The COVID-19 pandemic and its various aftereffects caused millions of people to wake up and rethink their lives. They began to question the morality of the standard business model, to reevaluate their priorities. Many realized that they could never again leave their future to chance, controlled by either employers or governments. They began to dream again, to crave for work that truly makes a difference. We're now in the era of the social entrepreneur, *and I believe this is going to propel a powerful growth era for leveraged sales.*

By joining leveraged sales, you benefit from a unique dynamic not found anywhere else: You work for yourself and control your own destiny—but also receive the support of a sponsorship line and company that have a vested interest in your success. As an independent distributor, you get to set the hours you work and choose the people you work with. You will be part of a community and meet people who may become friends for life. You will grow and learn new skills and have the chance to be exposed to and hang around successful people. You don't need prior experience or education. There are many tax benefits and travel opportunities. But there are two more benefits that are profound:

1. You have unlimited success potential. The only limit to where you end up is the size of your dream. (And being willing to put in the work.)
2. You become successful by helping other people reach success.

You've joined a profession that is making a positive difference in the world. We launch many innovative, breakthrough products that succeed only because of the conversational marketing we provide. We offer ordinary people the opportunity to unleash the wealth-building superpower of leverage, just like the super-rich. Most importantly, we offer people dignity by providing the ability to create an ongoing side income (and sometimes a full-time one) that allows them to escape poverty, provide for their loved ones, and build a better future.

We often hear about the huge incomes in our profession and become jaded. But never lose sight of the fact that there are millions of people on earth who have never flown on a plane, don't have enough to eat or safe water to drink, or subsist on substandard wages. Providing them a low-cost way to become an entrepreneur can transform their lives. And does. What you do *matters*. Congratulations! By being part of this movement, you've made a beneficial decision for us all.

Welcome to the Meritocracy

Another reason you've made such a savvy decision is the fact that leveraged sales is the ultimate meritocracy:

- Leveraged sales doesn't care whether you are highly educated or were expelled from high school (like me).

- Leveraged sales doesn't care if you're a trust-fund baby or down to your last dollar.

- Leveraged sales doesn't care if you have the prestige of royalty or your mom was a junkie.

- Leveraged sales will pay you exactly what you're worth—more specifically, the value you offer to your customers, distributors, and the world.

Distributors who mislead prospects, take advantage of their team, or jeopardize the profession are weeded out by the market. Initially it may seem like these people are successful achieving their desired goals. But they are building on sand and will soon collapse.

Tactics may draw people to you temporarily, but character will keep people with you. You might be able to cheat or game your way to the top of a network marketing company compensation plan, but your stay will be brief. You *remain* at the top by solving problems, adding value, and operating with integrity.

Leverage: The Superpower of Wealth Building

One of the most important talking points as you speak about your business should be *leverage*. The reason I call it a superpower for wealth is because it allows the average person to escape the trading-time-for-money trap that keeps millions broke. Study the world's greatest entrepreneurs and you'll notice they have one thing in common: They understand how to harness the power of *leverage*. Whether we look at business titans in the past like Rockefeller, Carnegie, and Ford—or the brilliant entrepreneurs of today such as Jeff Bezos, Oprah Winfrey, and Richard Branson—they've all built their wealth by employing the concept of leverage.

You need to show people that other side gig opportunities don't provide leverage like leveraged sales can. If you work for a food delivery app, but you're not delivering orders, you don't earn a penny. Working nights at a coffee shop provides some supplemental income, but no residuals. When you're working for a ridesharing app, but no calls come in, your bank account isn't growing.

In leveraged sales, you can create autoship customers that provide you with retail profits month after month. You can recruit and train others to do the same—and earn residual override income on the product volume created by their teams. It's the world's greatest opportunity for the average person without a college degree, large investment, or experience: the ability to unleash the power of leverage for themselves. Make sure you're getting that story out.

Know What You've Got

A big reason for the increasing acceptance and growth of leveraged sales comes from society steadily migrating toward the concept of people running part-time businesses on the side of whatever their job or profession might be. This trend is strongest among Millennials and subsequent generations. They love the idea of "side gig" or "side hustle" opportunities and have become a driving force in leveraged sales.

It's vital that you not only understand this side gig economy but know why leveraged sales offers people a dramatically superior option.

There are seemingly hundreds of side gigs you can work from home in your bunny slippers or Chewbacca pajamas: gamer, ecommerce and drop shipping, e-courses and other online education, graphic design, grant writing, recording audiobooks, un-boxing and reviewing, etc. Other side hustle opportunities involve putting on your shoes and getting dressed but still can offer good income potential: detailing cars, notarizing documents, flipping furniture, offering pet services, working for food delivery apps, and driving for rideshare companies.

Many of these other side gig models have done wonders for the economy, offering economic opportunities to millions of people who didn't have other viable options to transform their financial situations. Celebrate these models. And be able to articulate the primary advantages network marketing can offer over them.

Talk about *leverage* and *lifestyle*...

As mentioned above, for most of these side gigs, you're still snared in the trading-time-for-money trap. If you're not handing over the Moo Goo Gai Pan to apartment 3C, you ain't getting paid. If you're a rideshare driver, you're literally programming the software that will replace you the moment autonomous cars are legalized. With leveraged sales, you offer people the chance to unleash the power of leverage.

There are two other models worth exploring a little deeper…

Recently there's been an explosion of financially related side gig models: trading NFTs, forex, and crypto MLMs. The issues with these models are substantial. They include huge legal and financial risks, terrible duplication, and poor residual potential. Because these are such highly regulated areas, most of these models are often of questionable legality and frequently are outright fraud.

This takes us to the mother of all side gigs: becoming a digital content creator or online influencer. Often when I'm speaking to high school kids or young adults, this is their most desired occupation. After all, what could be cooler than working from home making zany videos, snagging sponsorship deals, and riding the computer algorithms to riches?

Um…not so quick…

For one in 10 million people, becoming an influencer provides life-changing money and a gratifying lifestyle. For the 9,999,999 others, they've unknowingly signed up for an earning model of high risks, terrible residual income, and zero security. Most online influencers are grinders, chasing both followers and sponsors, and continuously changing algorithms. If most influencers understood the lifestyle, income potential, security, and residual income potential of leveraged sales, they would shut down their accounts tomorrow.

When someone evaluates the whole spectrum of side gig opportunities, it's going to come down to an important question to ask…

How do you want to live?

Most people don't realize what a lonely and isolating job those other options can be: working alone, competing with everyone else who does what you do, hunting for secrets, paying for your education. When you recruit someone in your business, you're offering them the chance to become part of a greater team, with support and motivation from dreamers. You, their entire sponsorship line, and the company all have a vested interest in their success and will train and mentor them for free.

Know what you've got: Millennials and succeeding generations love side gig opportunities. Show them why you've got a better way.

Your Real Job

When you first begin in leveraged sales, you might think that your job is to sponsor everyone you know. That's not possible because each person makes their own decision whether to enroll or not. Instead, your job really is just this: to *prospect* everyone you know, meaning simply ask them to take a look.

You've been blessed with a great gift: an empowering way to earn a living and become successful by helping others reach success. That comes with a corresponding opportunity to share this gift with others. What they do with it is up to them.

What Duplicates > What Works

A lot of stuff works. What really matters is what *duplicates*.

If you run a commercial during the Super Bowl or World Cup, you could sign up tens of thousands of people. This strategy would work if you're just interested in collecting bodies. But how many of those new people would have the expertise and millions of dollars this requires to duplicate you?

Many people think duplication is about them and their techniques and tactics. They think they can muscle their way to duplication, but that never happens. Duplication cannot be pushed; it must be pulled. You must recruit and train people in a manner that illustrates how they can replicate the process so their people can replicate that process level after level after level…

You don't rise to the levels of your goals. You fall to the level of how duplicable your system is.

Beware of the Alligators

Fun fact: Alligators, who have one of the largest mouths you'll ever see, have a brain about the size of a lima bean. Unfortunately, there are people with the same ratio of mouth to brain dimensions. And they can't wait to tell you why leveraged sales is a scam, won't work, and that you're a loser for even trying.

Frequently they mean well. They're trying to protect you from something they're afraid could harm you. Frequently they don't mean well. They're attacking you from petty jealousy, because if you become successful, it takes away their excuse for the life of quiet desperation they live. It doesn't matter if their ignorance comes from a place of good intentions or not. If you buy into it, you'll sabotage your progress toward success.

You should know up front that you will encounter a few alligators, but they can be minimized by using tools to screen out people who aren't good prospects. You're also going to have prospects who don't show up for appointments and people who enroll only to drop out immediately afterward. People drop out of schools, marriages, and even life. This is all part of the spectrum of natural human behavior. The key is maintaining your equilibrium and staying focused on your dream.

When someone doesn't show for an appointment, a team member quits, or you come across an alligator, smile inwardly, and remind yourself that events like these are all part of the journey. And the journey is worth it. Never let someone who lost their dream steal yours.

Stop Chasing Antelopes

Never chase buses or candidates. There will always be another one along in a few minutes. If someone isn't interested, they won't become more so because you're hounding them.

One of the simplest philosophies is also one of the best: *Look for people who are looking.* If they're looking for a better life, you're looking for them. If they're not looking for a better life, you don't need to be looking for them, at least not right now.

Remember this isn't about closing and convincing but educating and opening. You never want to be presenting to anyone who doesn't want to be in a presentation in that moment. The secret is creating that anticipation. Don't chase people who are trying to run away. Let them paint their ass white and run with the other antelopes.

Book Two

Draft Your Superstars...

Follow the Formula

Success in our business is created by producing strong duplication. There is a three-part formula for creating duplication. And the closer you adhere to this formula, the stronger your duplication will be. Here it is:

Empower a large group of people to repeat a few simple actions over a sustained period of time.

Let's analyze the three parts...

Part one requires having a large enough group of people. If it's only you trying to empower one or two people, there's not enough traction to kick-start duplication. You need to keep recruiting until you have sufficient critical mass to start the process.

Part two involves getting the team to repeat a few simple actions. *Spoiler alert:* Learning neurolinguistic programming techniques is not a simple action. Becoming a social media influencer with 100,000 followers is not a simple action. Buying a $500 online study course to learn sales skills, how to overcome objections, and closing techniques is not a simple action.

When I say a few simple actions, I mean teaching people to do things like asking prospects to sample a product, review a booklet, or watch a presentation. The strongest growth is created when you drill down to the most basic elements, because every increase in complexity creates a corresponding decrease in duplication.

Finally, you've got to practice parts one and two for a long enough period to build out the culture of the organization. It you start out like a house on fire for two months then disappear for a few more, you'll come back to a dead or dying team. Stay consistent, following this formula religiously for your first year. After that your team will duplicate like it's on autopilot.

Learn the Parachute Skillsets

There are five parachute skillsets you need to become proficient in as quickly as possible. They are:

- Meeting People
- Working a Candidate List
- Inviting
- Presentations
- Follow-Up

I call these "parachute skills" because once you become proficient in them, you have earning skills that will always allow you to provide for your family. You could parachute into any free country—even one where you don't speak the language—and be able to earn a living. Ideally, everyone on the team will become proficient in these skills within your first few weeks, using the "study, do, and teach simultaneously" philosophy.

The most important thing to recognize early in your career is that all of these are skillsets, and skillsets can be learned and improved. When someone says, "I don't know that many people," what they're really saying is, 'I'm not willing to learn the skillset of meeting people."

Get the Convo Started

You already know that meeting people is a parachute skillset that can be learned. If you're naturally shy or introverted, this can seem to be a task too daunting. But you can easily short-circuit that fear by putting yourself in situations where others initiate conversations with you. And that happens when you are in environments of shared experiences.

If you're walking down the street wearing a *House of the Dragon* hoodie and someone is walking toward you in a *Game of Thrones* t-shirt, they probably can't wait to chat you up. When you're out walking Bella at 6AM and someone else is out with their pooch, you'll probably strike up a conversation effortlessly. And you can bet the keys to everything you own that if you're pregnant or pushing a baby stroller and encounter someone in the same situation, within three seconds you'll be chatting together like you've know each other for twenty years. Your shared experience creates an immediate bond. So, when you'd like to add some names to your candidate list, the best place to start is wondering where you might put yourself in a shared-situation experience. This can be anything from going to a comedy club or the midnight showing of a superhero movie premier to joining a sports league, taking an online class, or clicking on a hashtag.

Rinse and repeat, online and offline.

Fish Where the Fish Are

The anglers who catch the most fish don't accomplish that because they have some secret system to attract or catch fish. (Although most of them are liars and will say that they do.) The fishermen and women who catch the most fish do so because they fish where the most fish are. In our business this means you are always meeting new people and migrating them to your candidate list. And where do you find the most people today?

Online.

And you need to be online to meet them there. This doesn't mean you have to become an influencer with thousands of followers, take courses on how to attract followers, or become a content-creation factory. We can argue that those things are tough to duplicate anyway. But you still must at least have a presence online. You can meet people and prospect online organically. Just be sincere, be authentic, and be there.

Every generation from Millennials on are digital natives. They grew up on technology, live on their phones, and want businesses they can do online. When they're thinking about joining your team, one of the first things they do is search for you online. If your last post was on Myspace during the Bush administration, they may not feel that confident about your ability to lead a team today.

Of course, you can and will still meet plenty of people offline. But why limit your fishing to a local fishing hole and ignore the ocean?

Fish Where the Tasty Fish Are...

Not only do savvy fishermen fish where the fish are, but they go where the meaty, bigger fish are swimming, not the areas where the minnows congregate. In network marketing that means going after the best candidates first.

In fact, you should approach the most busy, most ambitious, most successful people on your list first. People who are successful in other jobs and businesses are likely to be successful in your business.

Don't make the mistake of not approaching those on your "chicken list"—the people you might be afraid to call because they have prestigious titles, a high level of education, or obvious wealth. The candidate who works two jobs, drives rideshare part-time, is a bishop in his/her church, coaches Little League, and volunteers at the soup kitchen will almost always find time to view your presentation. Meanwhile, you might find that your unemployed cousin living with his mom is too busy watching reruns of *Storage Wars* to listen to what you have to offer. People with good teaching or training skills (professors, speakers, coaches, yoga teachers, martial arts instructors, ministers, rabbis, imams, etc.) are naturals for the business.

You will find great candidates anywhere people of consciousness gather. Anyone who is working on themselves doing things such as continuing their education, taking courses, or attending seminars, learning another language, practicing self-development through books, blogs, or podcasts is a terrific candidate. All these things apply online or off. You might meet them in a bookstore (yes, they still exist) or on a website like Goodreads.com. You can meet great candidates at the deluxe car wash or art gallery—or in an online group or social media account about exotic cars or art.

Many spiritual communities like the Unity and Science of Mind Churches offer a wide variety of classes taught by instructors almost nightly. Gym classes like Zumba, Step, and Pilates as well. The people attending these courses are great candidates, and the ones who teach them might even be better. Pretty much every version of these live courses or classes has an online equivalent. Anyone who is doing anything to improve themselves—whether they are studying a foreign language, learning to draw, or taking up basket weaving—have a great potential to be a successful member of your team.

We've already talked about Millennials and the following generations. Because of their affinity for the side gig lifestyle, these upcoming generations are excellent candidates for you. (By the way, don't take this to mean you shouldn't be approaching Baby Boomers. There are outliers in every group. Boomers are used to hard work, stay committed, and don't want to outlive their money.)

We all know people who "need" the business desperately. But you should begin with the successful people on your list first. You'll develop skills, gain great experience, and start getting some financial results sooner. Then, by all means, go back to rescue those you want to help.

The best way to help the poor, sick, and exploited is to not be one of them.

Don't Be "That" Guy. (Or Gal)

The reason you learn the parachute skillsets is so you can recruit people in a process they'll be able to duplicate. Don't make the mistake of some new distributors who over-index on hype and start accosting every person they meet with a sales pitch. Your "commission breath" is going to repel them. There's also a time and a place for approaching people. Don't try to make a presentation to the guy in line behind you at the dry cleaner. Get his info and find a more suitable time and place. Don't invite people for dinner and just when they're expecting the cherry pie you pull out your tablet and launch your PowerPoint presentation.

Simply put, it's a lot better to be present and curious about them, ask questions, and monopolize the listening during dinner. If you do, you may find out their pains or dreams. You can always connect later with them and let them know they have been on your mind, and you have found something that can help them with their pains or dreams.

Likewise, when you are interacting online: You wouldn't walk down Main Street in your town, shouting at strangers to come to your presentation. So why would you do that on social media, through an email thread, or in a WhatsApp group?

There's a natural process that drives successful recruiting whether it's online or offline:

- Meet people
- Add to your candidate list
- Develop the relationship
- Approach when the timing is right
- Follow up as needed

Take More Shots on Goal

Some people appear to be naturals for the business, and almost everyone responds positively to their invitations. Other people appear to be terrible at the business, and everyone they approach runs away, shrieking in fear. But for 99 percent of the people in our business, their levels of success will be determined by two factors:

1. Their willingness to practice and improve on their parachute skillsets.
2. The number of people they approach.

The more shots on goal you take, the better your odds become of running up the score. Set aside a block of time every week and use it to invite candidates from your list to look at some kind of presentation: a physical tool, a livestream, or an in-person presentation.

Recruit for the 90 Percent, not the 10 Percent

Looking at the biz on the surface, it certainly appears to be a sales business. But that superficial view prevents you from seeing the whole picture. This is not just a sales business, it's a leveraged sales business. People who are great at sales receive only the minimal rewards of the business because their methods are hard to duplicate. The greatest results come when you're able to integrate teaching, duplication, and leverage.

Only about 10 percent of people have selling skills, leaving 90 percent who don't know how to sell, are deathly afraid of rejection, and wouldn't make a cold call if you held a gun to their head.

Think about the formula for duplication we discussed earlier. It begins with "Empower a large group of people…" Well, if you need a large group for success, which is the better crowd to draw from, the 10 percent or the 90 percent?

Viewed this way, your whole perspective expands. You begin to understand that while we get paid only for products or services that are sold to the end consumer—what causes those sales to multiply is duplication. So when you take the business as a whole, it's much more a teaching and training model, not a selling one.

Selling superstars from real estate or insurance can still be successful in the business. But this often requires a lot of training to show them how to avoid having their sales skills work against them. You certainly should give them the opportunity. But don't overlook the schoolteachers, yoga instructors, sports coaches, and others with strong teaching skills, because they are wonderful candidates for success. Likewise for engineers. Engineers think in terms of systems and analytics, so give them a duplicable system to follow and they can crush in the biz.

Big List = Strong Posture

In this context, posture doesn't mean standing up straight but the way you present yourself to candidates. Most importantly, the strength of your invitations. The foundation of our business is inviting. It requires inviting people constantly: to watch videos, listen to audios, read a booklet or brochure, or attend a presentation.

- A large candidate list produces a strong posture, which creates effective invitations.
- A small candidate list produces a weak posture, which creates ineffective invitations.

If you stop your list after the first five or six people you think are naturals for the business, you'll probably approach those people with a timid, fearful mindset, because if even a few don't get involved, you've already blown half your list. With a large list, you will approach people with more strength and confidence.

If there are 200 people on your list, you won't get despondent and worried if the first four aren't interested. You're still looking at 196 more, so it's a whole lot easier to stay positive and productive. A large list is the difference between begging people for favors instead of offering an opportunity with conviction. Candidates gravitate toward people with confidence.

The Law of the Drunken Orangutan

If you are in front of a candidate and your lips are moving—you need to be pointing to an external source tool.

You can spend years learning so much about your product/service line that you're able to make a compelling two-hour presentation to any candidate at any time. (You see this frequently in nutrition and wellness companies. Laypeople with no certification start diagnosing conditions and prescribing cures as though they were medical professionals. This is illegal, unethical, and dangerous.) If you take this route, you'll enroll lots of people, but most of them will quickly drop out. And the ones who remain will have low levels of duplication.

The same thing happens after you perfect your three-hour breakdown analysis of why your compensation plan is superior to any other plan ever developed. People will be impressed, many will sign up, but few will duplicate. These things look like an advantage on the surface but are duplication killers. Instead of learning a complex presentation, use an external source tool: a mobile app, flipchart, booklet, video, catalog, or some other resource.

If they're using the right external source tool, anyone, including a drunk orangutan, should be able to reach the first rank in your comp plan simply by pointing and grunting.

The "I Can Do This" Dynamic

When you make those amazing two- or three-hour presentations showcasing your expertise we just discussed, most candidates subconsciously will be thinking, "Wow, he/she knows a lot about this! I bet they're going to great in this business, but it would never work for me."

When you convey the benefits of your business using an external source tool, most candidates you make presentations to will subconsciously be thinking, "I could do this too."

Spoiler Alert: People who are thinking, "I could do this too," are usually the ones who sign up.

The Big Thing Is the Small Thing

You look at your phone and see it's a call from one of your new distributors. You answer to find them in breathless excitement over a special shortcut they've found to grow the business faster. You think you know where this is headed, but you let them share their breakthrough…

They explain that they just met the guy who styles the hair of the lady who walks the dog for the guy who washes Oprah's Bentley. And if you help them work the chain, they can enroll Oprah and she will sponsor 20,000 people a month. This is a big thing! Unfortunately, the big thing is the small thing, because the likelihood of this happening is almost zero.

Likewise, when you get a call from an excited distributor who just found out his brother-in-law works for the military in the procurement division. He thinks he's going to land a contract where they will buy your protein shakes for every soldier in the army. They have no idea of the multi-year bidding process and bureaucracy such a deal takes. And even given the minuscule possibility this deal gets done, it would produce sales but no duplication.

Here's the good news…

The small thing is the big thing. During the four years it might take to close that army contract, your distributor could instead focus on recruiting twelve or eighteen schoolteachers, rideshare drivers, little league coaches, plumbers, and stay-at-home moms (or dads) who follow the system and develop a team into 12,000 active distributors, who create a multimillion-dollar volume that produces residual overrides for decades.

The big thing is the small thing, and the small thing is the big thing.

Open People, Don't Close Them

Isaac Newton gave us three Laws of Motion:

1. An object at rest remains at rest, and an object in motion remains in motion at constant speed and in a straight line unless acted on by an unbalanced force.
2. The acceleration of an object depends on the mass of the object and the amount of force applied.
3. Whenever one object exerts a force on another object, the second object exerts an equal and opposite on the first.

Allow me to add a fourth:

4. The harder you close someone, the less they will duplicate.

People you must manipulate or arm-twist to join will buy a starter kit but will also be the first ones to drop out. Stop closing people and start opening them. Meaning simply present your case in the most honest but compelling way. Educate your candidate on all the benefits they will receive from your product line and business opportunity, then let them make what they feel is the best decision for them.

If that means being a customer, great. If that means joining the business, great. If that means not joining in any capacity, great. Honor the no. By doing that, if later their situation changes and the timing is better, you have a much better shot at getting a new customer or distributor. You'll enroll fewer people, but you'll have a much more active team and a much more fulfilling life.

RANDY GAGE | 39

Book Three

Leading an All-Volunteer Army...

Hard Truth

There's only one cause for a bad team, and that's a bad leader.

Own it.

Study. Do. Teach.

Most people who join our leveraged sales profession begin their career by doing something that looks like the ideal way to reach success but is actually a terrible mistake, causing slower growth for them and their team.

What is this harmful mistake?

They think that first they should *study* the business, so that later they can *do* the business, and even later, *teach* the business. They want to study everything for two months first. Then they believe they will act. And then, once they are rich and famous, they'll go back and train everyone on how to achieve their level of success.

Of course, this scenario works only in fantasy. Because if you model this timeline, then the people you bring in duplicate that process and growth takes too long. The time required for people to earn anything of substance is so drawn out that your dropout rate spikes dramatically.

Motivation and positive thinking will carry a new distributor only so far. Unless a person has a believable, logical plan for attaining her dreams, fear and procrastination will take over. If someone studies the business for weeks, and only then starts doing it, they're usually not still around later to teach it. This dramatically alters the DNA of your team because everyone takes their lead from the behavior you modeled for them initially.

To create rapid, strong, and sustained success, you need to study, do, and teach simultaneously.

Sounds crazy, but it's easier to build the business fast than it is to build slowly. Starting fast creates excitement and momentum that spreads down your group. And by generating cash flow quickly, you set the tone for your team and create an exciting demonstration of success for candidates. If you spend your first few weeks "getting ready to get ready," you'll probably find yourself on a procrastination train. Your excitement fades and your dream gets further away.

I believe you make or break a new distributor in the first two weeks, and the first forty-eight hours are critical. The goal is that someone can join on a Tuesday, go through their new distributor orientation that night, and be enrolling customers and distributors within their first two days. Then help their new distributors replicate the process. This keeps getting duplicated on every level and creates an ever-expanding ripple effect throughout the team. The result is strong DNA throughout the team, creating a vicious cycle of growth and duplication.

Help Real People in the Real World

There are so many people in our profession who are earning five- and six-figure monthly checks that we sometimes get jaded. (I once had a guy jump from my team to another company because he felt he was a failure—because he was only earning $50K a month.)

In most of the world, you can transform someone's life with a supplemental, residual income of a few hundred dollars or euros a month. It's okay to dream big and shoot for those big checks, bonus cars, and exotic trips. Just know that the best way to attain them is a grounded approach to help as many people as possible get out of debt and start building a healthy financial future for their families.

How Does It Play 25 Levels Down?

Before you make any big change in an approach, ask yourself the following question: *How well could this action I'm about to take be duplicated by somebody twenty-five levels below me, who has never met me in person?*

They probably know your name, maybe they've seen you on stage at a convention or on a livestream. But if they haven't met you, will they get the same results as you?

Don't Confuse Reactive with Active

Let's suppose you're working with a wellness company. One afternoon you're on break with a co-worker from your day job and he complains about feeling tired in the afternoon. You leap into action, providing information about your company's amazing energy drink. Your co-worker places an order, so you pat yourself on the back for doing such a great job, actively building your business.

Not so fast…

Now suppose you are out for dinner with friends and one of them mentions that she doesn't like her job because the pay is low and offers little potential for advancement. Again, you leap into action and invite her to see an opportunity presentation. Like the previous example, you did something that can grow your business. That's great, but these gains happened only because the candidates were practically begging you for information. That's being reactive—don't confuse that with being active. You want to be active and intentional about growing your business.

This means that every week you should have a block of time in your schedule, exclusively dedicated to contacting candidates, inviting them to look at what you have to offer.

Cutting Edge = Off the Ledge

For many of you reading this, at some point in your lifetime you're going to be able to purchase a robot or software that will be able to:

- Make 100 billion calculations per second.
- Scour social media, broadcast networks, and employment databases, identifying ideal candidates for your business.
- Give you an accurate probability percentage as to who will respond positively to a presentation, eliminating any chance of rejection.
- Scan your candidates while you make presentations—monitoring their breathing and pulse rates, eye movements, and body language, sending you signals when your points are resonating with them.

If you can be the first person on earth to purchase that software, let me tell you what will happen:

- You will become the number-one recruiter in your company.
- Most likely you will recruit more people than anyone else in history.
- You will make a ton of cash, have the worst duplication of any leader, and become very frustrated and unfulfilled. You will likely drop out within a year, knowing that there are better and more effective ways to utilize your robot.
- As your last act before you quit, you'll buy 400,000 copies of this book and gift them to the team members you left behind to assuage your guilt for unknowingly exploiting them.

There are lots of well-meaning (and, unfortunately, a few not very well-meaning) people who will be trying to sell you courses, coaching programs, and e-books on how to recruit using the latest and greatest cutting-edge technology. But remember the formula for duplication we discussed earlier. You want to lead your team to do a few simple actions. So, in the case of leveraged sales, anything bleeding edge or even leading edge is going to murder your duplication results.

It's Easier to Give Birth Than Resurrect the Dead

No matter how hard you try, or how bad you want it for someone else, you can't drag them across the finish line. It's like trying to push a rope. And the worst part is that often they will be trying to pull you back into being a victim. It is not your job to build the businesses for other people, this is their responsibility. If it's to be, it's up to them. Lead by example, offer support, and be there for them, but they must walk the path.

Stop chasing alligators, antelopes, and people who desperately want to remain a victim. Put a wreath on the coffin and go find someone who wants to live their dream.

Chill on Your Personal Brand, Bro

Don't try to make yourself the superhero. Superhero leaders who want to build up their personal brand all the time suck all the oxygen from the room. This starts a progression of decreasing duplication and increasing grinding. You may think you look good in a cape and tights, but you're going to end up on a reality TV show wondering why you're surrounded by so many co-dependent people.

Make the team, the system, and the lifestyle we offer the superhero. *This isn't about building people's belief in you but building belief in themselves.*

Any time you have a choice of being famous or being rich—choose rich.

Action Is the Answer

Most people don't need bigger goals or a larger vision—they need to take more action. The answer to all the biggest challenges in your business is action.

- If you don't know enough people, the answer is action.
- If your volume is too low, the answer is action.
- If you're not qualifying at rank, the answer is action.
- If your group seems lethargic and lazy, the answer is action.
- If two of your leaders are at war, the answer is action.
- If the economy is creating stress on your product sales, the answer is action.
- If a bunch of products are on backorder, the answer is action.
- If another company is poaching your people, the answer is action.
- If your sponsor is a jerk, the answer is action.

Lift People's Eyes Above the Horizon

A couple decades ago, I was asked to give my definition of leadership for a book on that subject. I defined it then as the ability to cause people to willingly take actions they wouldn't normally want to do. (Example: In a war, someone charges a machine gun nest to protect their unit. In our business, it may be as simple as someone buying their first suit or giving their first presentation in front of a group.)

My thinking has evolved, and here is how I would define leadership today:

Inspiring people to become the highest possible version of themselves—and building the environment that facilitates this process.

Managers work from power and authority. They can force people to do things because of the control they hold over issuing paychecks. Leaders must work from inspiration, causing people to willingly choose to take action.

The best leadership skills I developed for leveraged sales came from outside the business. What helped me most was the work I did serving on boards for my church, the chamber of commerce, a film festival, etc. Because in each case I was working with an all-volunteer army. When you can't hire and fire people, you're forced to learn how to inspire, lead, and partner with them for achieving a common goal. That's what will make you great in this business.

Cause and Effect

To create a better life, you must create a better you. The difference between your group today and your group ten years from now will be the books you read, the podcasts you listen to, and the people you associate with. Your business will grow only as fast as you do.

Making Moves...

Place your individual attention on people who show they are motivated and working and use group training to work with the rest. A productive relationship between a sponsor and a team member is like a chess match: You make a move, they make a move, you make the next move, and so on. Don't make two moves in a row.

Don't Be a Helicopter Sponsor

Have you seen helicopter parents who hover over their children constantly, desperately seeking to protect them from ever scraping their knees? Have you seen how those kids end up? Never do anything for a distributor they can do themselves or you're hurting their development.

Shut Down the All-You-Can-Eat Buffet

Don't give away personal enrollees, do the work your team members are supposed to be doing, or place orders to qualify them at rank. You're creating a dysfunctional culture that not only won't duplicate but will create entitlement mentality.

Teach people how to fish. If they demand the all-you-can-eat fish fry, direct them to another restaurant.

Tell Your Story in a Way That Empowers

If you get invited to speak at a convention or other major event, you might think it's a reward for your hard work. It's not; the pin and bonus check are for that. You're being asked to share your story in a way that empowers the whole team.

No one wants to hear an entire speech about all the bonus cars, award trips, and huge checks you've earned. When you're given the privilege of the platform, use it to show the audience you have been where they are, and you can guide them to get to where they want to be.

Lose the Lambos

Back in the day, our recruiting pitch was simple: lots of pix of voluptuous young women in bikinis, stacks of cash, and exotic supercars. (I wouldn't know anything about this of course!) There are two reasons you shouldn't recruit that way any longer:

1. It's tacky.
2. It doesn't work anymore.

Sensibilities have changed. Back when Michael Douglas won an Oscar for portraying the fictional character Gordon Gekko with his "greed is good" monologue in the movie *Wall Street*, this type of rah-rah approach was not just tolerated but frequently emulated. Although such tactics can work with a small subsection of the population today, they're not the people you want on your team.

Focus your message on social entrepreneurship, getting people out of debt, and becoming successful by helping other people reach success. It works. And it's the right thing to do. (And if you still want a Lambo, you'll get it faster.)

Challenge, Don't Pander

People like to be told what they want to hear. Unfortunately, that doesn't serve them. If you really want to help the people on your team, love them enough to challenge them to become the highest possible versions of themselves.

Search for Greatness

The greatest gift you can give the people on your team is to see the greatness in them before they see it in themselves. Then tell them. They might just borrow your belief in them until they develop it for themselves.

Expect Greatness

Treat every new distributor as if they have the potential to reach the highest rank in the company, unless and until they prove it otherwise.

Build a Dream Greater Than the Team

No matter how large the bonus checks get, how expensive the bonus cars become, or what caret diamonds are in the bling-bling, at some point the sugar rush is just empty calories. The material rewards of our business are delicious, but the best reward is who you become.

The greatest leaders in our space elevate people's eyes above the horizon. Inspire people to become part of something greater than themselves.

Be the Kind of Sponsor You Would Want

When someone enrolls with you, they're giving you a sacred honor. Do everything you can to deserve that trust.

- Never knowingly lie to them.
- Don't advise them of anything not in the best interest of their business (not yours).
- Direct them through a New Distributor Orientation.
- Have them enroll for the free *Duplication Nation Alerts* at https://duplicationnation.com/
- Make sure they read this book.
- Let them borrow your belief until they develop their own.

You Have a Responsibility to Be Successful

You can't help anyone break rank, earn big bonus checks, or reach the top of your compensation plan until you've done it yourself. Only then can you become an empowering sponsor, coach, and mentor.

You are responsible to model the appropriate behavior and showcase what a well-managed distributorship looks like. Have a viable customer ratio, keep enrolling, demonstrate exemplary event participation, and work in depth. You owe it to your team to get out of debt, run a profitable business, and live a dream lifestyle. Be the change you seek.

When It's Not Working...

When your enrollments and volume seem to plateau, or you seem to be encountering excessive friction, here's a checklist of questions to consider:

- Am I doing the actions I want my distributors to do?
- How can I be a little better tomorrow?
- Where can I look it up?
- Am I following the system, or did I go rogue?
- What book should I read to break out now?
- Who can I ask in the sponsorship line?
- How would Randy handle this situation?
- Who are the three best candidates I can contact right now?

Be the #1 Investor in Your Dream

If you don't invest in yourself, you're probably a bad investment for anyone else. What are you doing to invest in your health, develop new skillsets, learn more about the business, and become a stronger leader?

Here's the million-dollar question…

What do you spend more on each week—your self-development or Starbucks?

Ride the Tide

It's been said that a rising tide raises all boats. That's true, but the concept only works if your boat is in the water. If you allow challenges or rejection to make you quit, your boat goes into drydock. Never give up on your dreams.

Decide

Success is a decision. When you make a decision, you can turn around and create a new direction in any area of your life.

No matter where you are right now, it doesn't have to be the same after today. You can do the most extraordinary things. You can transform your life at any moment. But only when you decide to.

Final Thoughts: You Are Worth It

Leveraged sales is simple, but it's not easy. In fact, the business can be tough sometimes. Let's go back to where we started. You're going to face alligators, dropouts, and no shows—and rejection, apathy, and even ridicule. But don't ever give up because the challenges are worth it. The work is worth it. *You're* worth it.

People without a dream are threatened by those who still have one. For every person seeking greatness, there are hundreds more whose job is safeguarding mediocrity. Please. Stop trying to fit in.

Be bold. Be a dreamer. Be a dreamer so bold, that if you ever get charged for the crime of dreaming, there's enough evidence for the jury to convict you.

Peace,

— RG

Contract With Myself

I commit to making this year the year that will transform my life. This is my contract to my higher self, the person I am meant to become. Here are my commitments:

1) I will work my business with passion, intensity, and urgency.
Allowing for two weeks of vacation, I will work at least ten hours a week during the other fifty weeks in committed, productive activities to grow my business.

2) I will model a prosperous lifestyle.
I will strive to live my life and build my business in a way that will inspire my team.

3) I will become financially free.
Each month I will move toward erasing debt and becoming debt-free.

4) I will lead my team to victory.
A victory is not my rank or goal. Victory is helping the prosperity warriors on my team reach their true potential. My victory comes from helping them achieve theirs. I will not simply watch the movement. I will be the movement.

5) I will not give up.
I will face my fears and summon courage. When others doubt me, I will remember why I began this journey. When people reject me, ridicule me, or attack me, I will use that as fuel to build strength. I will stand strong for my dreams. On this, I will never compromise. I deserve success and prosperity and will not give up until I achieve it.

This is my contract with myself.

Date: _____ Signature: _____

(You may want to take a photo of this and send to your sponsor.)

Mad Love to:

…**Jaime Lokier,** my co-warrior at DuplicationNation.com where we're working to take the profession back from the con artists and scammers who are trying to hijack the business.

…my work wife, the lovely and talented **Ann Feinstein**, who is always there when I need her.

…**Steven Pressfield,** for being my friend, for being brilliant, and for writing *The War of Art,* which served as the inspiration for this book.

…The leaders and execs you see at the start of the book who were gracious enough to provide a review. Extra gratitude for those who critiqued the very first outline, providing sage advice and suggestions for making this book more helpful for you and your team. They include: **Ørjan and Hilde Saele, Jordan Adler, Jeremiah Bradley, Peter Andreas Sørensen, Dana Collins, Michael Smith, Andi Duli, John Solleder, Jose Lopez,** and **the Duke of Chigwell: His Royal Highness Wesley Hawthorn Harrison Linden III**. And a supersized dollop of appreciation for **Erick "Flaco" Gamio,** who was the toughest on me—and thus the most helpful.

…**Vicki McCown,** likely to go down in history as the greatest book editor since the Earth's crust cooled.

…**Joey "Jojo" Leslie,** the guy who keeps me out of the ditches and who, along with **Devan Horning, Crystal Andrus,** and the crack commando team at Prime Concepts Group, brought this book to the world.

…**My mom,** who raised three kids by herself, knocking on doors selling AVON products. The best role model for success a future entrepreneur could ever have.

About the Author...

If you want to reach success in leveraged sales, there is probably no one on Earth better qualified to help you than **Randy Gage**. An icon of the profession, Randy helped introduce the business in many developing countries and has trained the top income-earners in dozens of companies. Randy teaches from real-world experience, having earned millions of dollars as a distributor, and built a team of more than 200,000 people.

Randy is the author of fifteen books translated into more than twenty-five languages, including the *New York Times* best-sellers, *Risky Is the New Safe* and *Mad Genius*. He has spoken to more than two million people across more than fifty countries and has been inducted into the Speaker Hall of Fame. When he is not prowling the platform or locked in his lonely writer's garret, you'll probably find him batting cleanup for a softball team somewhere.

DuplicationNation.com

Your trusted source for generic leveraged sales training and information curated by Randy Gage and Jaime Lokier. A powerful resource to grow your team. Be sure to sign up for the free *MLM Boot Camp* email course and *Duplication Nation Update*. You'll receive a new issue every week, including some actionable content that will help you build your volume, recruit better, or develop your leadership skills. We know you're busy so this content will be in the form of tips, short essays, or other easy-to-digest methods. You'll also receive a free copy of the *Rapid Start Guide*.

Recommended Resources:

What you're reading now is really a "why to" book. If you want the ultimate "how to" book on leveraged sales, read Randy's *Direct Selling Success: From Amway to Zombies*.

This book will show you how to:

- Choose the right company for you
- Become a Rock Star recruiter
- Design your system for maximum duplication
- Prospect brilliant talent
- Create a leadership factory on your team
- Build around the country (or the world) effectively
- Conduct powerful, persuasive presentations
- Construct a "bullet proof" duplicable system
- Become a positive, dynamic leader for your team!

For Top Leaders...

Many people believe leadership in leveraged sales means being positive all the time, sending lots of happy emojis to your WhatsApp groups, and giving motivational speeches. But the truth is, the "unicorns and rainbows" perspective is only a small part of true leadership. Because true leadership deals with the messy, complicated, and dark areas as well.

Many of the challenges you might face are caused by factors completely out of your control, and there isn't always a clear-cut solution. Economies falter, top leaders quit, and companies go out of business. How do you stay true to your principles and lead the team forward when their world is falling apart because of a comp plan change, regulatory attacks, or a competitor poaching away top leaders?

DEFCON 1 Direct Selling will teach you how to:

- Deal with toxic leaders and effectively handle conflict resolution
- Navigate regulatory attacks and negative publicity
- Work around corporate incompetence or poor decisions
- Protect against dangerous team dynamics
- Respond when a top leader leaves the company

Duplication Nation MLM Podcast

If you're in network marketing, leveraged sales, or direct selling—this is the podcast you always wanted! Randy Gage and Jaime Lokier, curators of DuplicationNation.com, share their insights on how you build volume, strengthen duplication, increase recruiting, and develop your leadership skills. Subscribe and receive a new episode every Tuesday. Watch for special episodes where Randy chops it up with a top leader about the behind-the-scenes subjects you won't hear anywhere else. Find it on YouTube and all the major podcast platforms.

MLM Confidential

The Private Subscribers-Only Newsletter for Million-Dollar Earners and the People Who Aspire to Become One

MLM Confidential is a private members-only newsletter for million-dollar earners and C-suite company executives. (And people who aspire to become a member of one of those groups.) It's not for MLM zombies who flit from deal to deal, the dinosaurs waiting for the computer fad to pass, or the criminals promoting MLM crypto scams or other Ponzi schemes. It is only for distributors who are deadly serious about building a multi-million-dollar residual income from their leveraged sales business. (Although company owners, marketing directors, and other corporate executives will find it quite helpful as well.)

This is a powerful resource that will show you how to dramatically increase your income, develop stronger duplication in your team, and create a true passive income that will continue long after you stop working. It's elite-level coaching and guidance from two of the most successful people to ever click through a PowerPoint presentation in our profession: **Randy Gage** and **Jaime Lokier.** They've locked arms for the first time to offer leadership mentoring at a level never seen before in the network marketing/leveraged sales profession.

Subscribe at: https://www.mlmconfidential.com/subscribe